# Harm's
# Way

# Harm's Way

## Maureen Hynes

Brick Books

CANADIAN CATALOGUING IN PUBLICATION DATA

Hynes, Maureen
Harm's way

Poems.
ISBN 1-894078-14-4

I. Title.

PS8565.Y63H37 2001    C811'.54    C2001-930055-7
PR9199.3.H96H37 2001

We acknowledge the support of the Canada Council for the Arts
for our publishing programme. The support of the Ontario Arts
Council is also gratefully acknowledged.

The cover image is 'Sand Castle' by Jean-François Bérubé, 1998.
The author's photo is by Greg Staats.

Typeset in Minion. The stock is acid-free Zephyr Antique laid.
Printed and bound by The Porcupine's Quill Inc.

Brick Books
431 Boler Road, Box 20081
London, Ontario N6K 4G6

brick.books@sympatico.ca

For Terry, Gerry, Joanne

# Contents

11   Harm's Way

## Risk insurance

15   Precaution
16   The molecular level of kindness
17   Lie perfectly still. Turn on the light.
19   Waterman's Fountain Pen
20   Storks of Kampala
22   When Dili was on fire
23   Dance Pavilion
24   Irish Literature Exam
26   My Great-Grandmother's Hands
27   The Careful Things
28   Christmas on the Otonabee
29   Driving into the Blizzard
32   That night in June at the farmhouse

## The whitewashed oval of a roadside grotto

35   Event Horizon
36   Speechless
37   *Las Calaveras*
39   Yellow Parachute
40   The High Salt Content of His Tears
43   Old Hall Light
44   Nine New Undershirts
45   In Paradisum
46   Estate
48   Chac Mool
50   In the Bottom of the Boat

## The alphabet of what's given and received

53   Panorama
54   One Corpse

55  Fossils, Brachina Gorge
56  Stone Sofas
57  Cypress Fire
58  After Burn-Out
59  Sand Dunes
60  Desert Rainfall
61  The road closes and opens
62  Corrugated Iron
63  Junk Jewellery
64  Broken Glass
65  Target Practice

The first three times were scorching

69  Horoscope
70  Upside-Down Cake
71  Clang
72  This, then, is the snow-filled track
73  Cold Feet Hotel
74  Lip-Synching, Two Performances
76  First Symptoms
79  When the face of the former beloved
81  Six Tulips
82  What Dreams Assume
85  Two Weak Arms
86  Lunar Eclipse

89  Notes on the poems

91  Acknowledgements

What is our innocence,
what our guilt? All are
        naked, none is safe. And whence
is courage: the unanswered question,
the resolute doubt –

Marianne Moore, 'What are Years?'

# Harm's Way

*Some of us wear a piece of the road as an amulet*
*over our breastbones: may harm not wind its way back to us.*

*The first three times were scorching, you can feel*
*the small disc of heat on your chest. Risk insurance.*

*A woman draws a yearly bucket of water from*
*the well a child drowned in, makes a thin soup*

*for her family. A girl braids silk threads to tie*
*around her wrist, while the boy shatters birds' eggs,*

*pierces and threads two fragments to hang*
*around his neck, front and back, like a scapular.*

There's that noise again.

Some kind of a basement noise, but you're outdoors.
Your ears flinch, your eyes sharpen into the dusk.

Striding down the gravel shoulder in your too-new Reeboks
and far off, a zamboni, a cyclone, a minotaur.

Alone but that's okay. Until now. Fragile suddenly
and thunderstruck. Peel your hands off your throat

and scream, why don't you scream? Jump into the field,
into the hay with the rest of the sneezes. Turn back, tear

down the road to your rumpled bed. No, stay still and listen
for the frogs or the stars falling out of the dusk.

This is Harm's Way and no escaping, no Tahiti or
Bora Bora for you, no flights to and from,

no slipping out or nodding off, no sitting around

singing sad songs, Goodnight Irene, Swing Low Sweet Chariot.

This is harm's way, the traffic ahead is bad. Bulldozers
heaping and curling a wave of hazards and the loudest trouble

is distilled into something tiny and deep, the first kiss
of breast milk ticks with odds, one in nine, one in three.

This map's no good, takes you right into the nuclear plant.
Good paved road, the forest's cleared, the atoll's bald.

Melanoma or divorce or stroke or military coup
chugging its particular noise directly toward you, no

signature required. Oh, says your mother,
that's just harm's way of telling you to get out of the road.

– That's all right, she says tenderly from aloft. She brushes
your hair and strengthens the terror. Stretches and thins it.

Summoned or shunned doesn't matter, no pleading
a special case, no spreading laurels to rest beneath,

privileges peel off and crackle, a stained old pair
of evening gloves. The rosary mumbles its beads.

You search overhead, clouds dull the moon's faint glow.
Why is this road so empty when you know you're not alone,

why is it always night on this particular stretch?
Rip a poncho out of your pack, spread it on the dark wet weeds,

lean against the whitewashed oval of a roadside grotto,
and recite the alphabet of what's given and received.

Here's a thread of dawn. Tie your shoelaces, scramble on.

# Risk
## insurance

# Precaution

Three hours of hesitant driving
along guardrails in the cold coastal rain
and the houses staring with a certain closed
belligerence. The isolation, each from each.
Pull over. Step out of the car, stretch your
arms and legs against the salty details
of the rain, lean against the car door,
finish your cooling coffee.

Just inside the brown slat fence, two small girls
stand in a packing crate.
Their eyes and arms brim its edge.
'This is our spaceship,' says the younger one,
maybe four years old.
You ask her, 'And where are you taking it?'
'To New York, and the moon and the sun
and all the stars.' Across the field,
from the doorway of his house
a man calls to them. You watch him stride
across the wet meadow in his black rubber boots,
the same orange band around their rims
as your brothers' boots when they were paperboys.
He summons them from the box, takes each
by a hand and hurries them back across the field
into the house.

A welter of words has died on your lips, mostly
yes and no. Wild irises, stunted by the cold
salt air, grow at the edge of the wet grass.
You get back in the car, drive
up the twisting ocean road to the lighthouse.

## The molecular level of kindness

a tiny piston that fires in every fibre
poops out and you barely
notice, you function fine
without it, the car still makes
its turns, though the indicator light
doesn't go on anymore: you don't return
a message for days, it gets automatic, warding
off too many calls; you neglect a birthday
card (oh, well, she's not a child); the mother
unvisited in her dementia, your cells refuse
another obligation to your father; the colleague
barely greeted, and you recall the particular
argument – it was about Palestine –
when you first understood
the aggression of your own silence;
not to mention the unspoken refusal
in that telephone conversation
where the moments spread out like stepping-stones
from which to jump and splash and spin
and what had been kindness released unkindness

it's mostly in what you don't do, weary,
inattentive, preoccupied with a headache,
declining the effort of conversation
how silence becomes a habit – a fearful habit or just
laziness, you can't quite figure which – that overlays

the transitory miracle, the man who asked
for a sandwich and you had one to give,
the newcomer's delight in your precise
directions to the best lakeside view

                                        you keep
forgetting to put spare
change in your pocket for the street people

## Lie perfectly still. Turn on the light.

Middle of the night, tires spinning
against the slight icy rise of my street
awaken me. Again and again the car
roars a climbing octave
up to my window, then falls
defeated, roars and falls.

I have been swimming in the dark seawater of dreams
and now my body contains the dream as a shore
contains a lake. I hold the dream rippling
in my arms, rest my head against
its lapping. Lie perfectly still.

Lie perfectly still. Reach out. Turn on the light.
Pull the notebook and pen onto the bed, and write.
My curious custom of hurrying slowly to stay right here.

I am back in China. Already the dream is spilling.
We are outside the gates of the university
setting out for a bike ride along the river.
It is summer and we have scattered
our bicycles on the pavement behind us.
We are discussing how strange
and uneven the wall is now, and the brilliant
red characters (I cannot read them)
carefully painted on its white stucco.
And there, just out of sight, beyond the gates,
the wall turns into a curtain
that shimmers and lifts in the wind
like some kind of metal mesh.
My young friends are Chinese, but they can't explain
the writing on the wall. I am not holding a lake,
not talking to my friends,
I am writing in my notebook.

I get out of bed, look out of the window,
the taxi drives off, the dream falls to the floor,
my body is dripping with lakewater
two lines of black ice scarred into the road.

# Waterman's Fountain Pen

*A farmer ploughing his field unearthed the remains of a First World War
French soldier, 29-year-old Alexandre Villedieu, whose fountain pen was still
full of ink 81 years after he was killed ...*
      *'After a few tries, I could still write with it,' said Alfred Duparq, president of
the local historical association. 'It was beautiful, like old-fashioned
writing.'   The* Globe and Mail, *April 20, 1996*


In the afternoon, you will write them all.
After the dawn shelling and the mustard gas,
before the phosphorescence cracks the night apart again,
you will write; your Waterman's pen is full of beautiful
words, old-fashioned words like *espoir* and *promesse* and *demain*.
Sit down over there, just past the shellshock and stretchers,
past the trees scorched leafless in May,
past the trenches shin-high with a thin soup of mud.

Your pen defeats the mud. Tell me
who you would have written, the young Italian
sculptor you met at art college, the *téléphoniste*
back home, the *jeune maîtresse* who took over
the village school, of course your mother
– whose lives did you enter through
this gold nib, thin as a bayonet?

Blood spilled, ink contained. Your words
unwritten but ready. A spiritualist
could get her hands on that pen,
and after a few tries, write your last letter,
your reminders, your remains.

## Storks of Kampala

*Uganda, 1985*

In the early morning, a massive bird attacks
our window: close-up of claws, huge wings flapping,
its pointed beak and pendulous throat sac
on a long bare neck – an image of terror, framed
and hanging in our hotel room.

I remember a baby's room back home:
above her crib, a blurred photo of storks nesting
in a European chimney. Here
they look like vultures, perched
on window ledges above the piles of garbage
simmering on every street corner. Grimy
sentinels, they keep watch
over the rotting stew of fruit peels and cellophane
for the quick dart, a rat, a mouse.
How can you run your shop,
I asked a hairdresser, no water or electricity
until dusk? We pay, she said, we pay.

Yesterday the hotel owner told us to come back
in exactly three hours, before the curfew.
We spent the afternoon with the taxi drivers
under the acacias in the railway station's park.
Could we imagine its perimeter lined with corpses –
starting with the edge of the parking lot,
could we get further than the torn clothing,
dried blood, arrested flail of arms and legs
in the larger heap, pile the mounds
all the way to the red brick station? –
                                        no.

In the evening we looked down from the hotel room
onto the park, a yellowing clockface
spread below us, eight dusty paths radiating
from its centre. We settled in the damp, half-
painted room, the iron bed swallowed
into the corner, our packs open on the floor.
A thin trickle of cold water to wash
my hair as I knelt in the tub. In the suburbs,
machine-gunfire burst out at the stars. That night,
the phone in the railway station rang
steadily for four hours. How could we sleep?
But we did, until the stork woke us, we slept
through the sweet smell of garbage
burning and extinguished and burning –
a wasted, desultory conversation with the rain.

## When Dili was on fire

The child heard the thin ascending vibrato of the nighttime cicadas
and mistook them for the noise the stars make:
by the tenderness required to unhook, reconnect his understanding
an entire motherhood is made worthwhile. At what age do we
accept the stars' silence, only then to learn their calls are sent,
arrive in other galaxies or future centuries? Now what I hear
is an enormous cold patience from within those dots, those blurs;
what I see are flickers of recognition as East Timor is burning
down to the ground – soon our place
in the night sky will be shrouded in smoke,
the faint outcry will be ours,
a sharpening two-note call of alarm and loss.

# Dance Pavilion

*Manitou Lake, Saskatchewan*

Inside the van, they consider the approach
of sunset; quiet laughter
as the road, straight-pinned onto the prairie,
pegs its way forward like a curtain seam
spilling out of an old sewing machine. Overhead,
muted calls and the sharp angle of the geese's flight
widens, splinters, tightens. Then the van

turns the only bend of the trip,
the bend that hugs the sudden
low hills still etched with tipi rings, the bend
that rims and crosses the salt water lake
in the middle of this province of pelicans
and grid roads, arches and softens the evening,
releases it with the bounce, bounce, bounce

of a let-go ball of yarn. Under
the dancehall's rounded roof,
greyed and graceful couples
move in circles on the sprung floor,
the O's of the saxophones
surround them, *My Blue Heaven,*
the vocabulary of nostalgia
– console radio, they think, sunset and the quarter moon;
dance us back to Casa Loma, the hotel suite
at war's end, that return and the stories
sealed for decades. O, the fidelity
of the pavilion, and the old bandleader's skill.

At the edge of the polished maple dance floor,
two young women in thin dresses and Doc Martens hold
each other gingerly, we'll learn this here,
try out our affection. Is this, then, how injuries
are healed?

## Irish Literature Exam

I failed the exam, couldn't
finish it. Three essay questions.
This one would be easy, I knew the book so well,
as if I lived three cottages
down from Eileen Sean, as if I knew her
and her husband the fisherman who would play
only the one tune on the penny whistle,
and her son, Eoine, nine years old, fallen
a hundred feet over the cliff.
Around me in the huge hall,
twenty rows of students coughing
and writing page after furious page.
I write on my scrap paper, *I am not
on the west coast of Ireland, I am in Canada.*

The woman's scream
fells her; flat on her stomach,
she sees his small back hit the rocks,
his fists and eyes still grabbing up to her
and the waves pull him out fast, not a minute
gone and there's no sight of him, his red jumper,
his black boots. Throwing his name down
after him down the cliff,
and I am screaming too, running for the old men
to get out in their curraghs.

Was it a quick loop of wind
that curled up over the cliff to snatch him,
or was it a mighty wall that came storming
behind and gave him the one push? For two days
the men searched for him, their cries tattered
and swallowed into the wind. The accident of ocean
and he's lost.

Two nights and days
full of a gouging wind; you could hear it
scrape at the cliffs like a breadknife, pulverizing
the waves below into a spume so cold
the droplets scoured and stung the limestone ledges.
Inside the cottage the fire was dropping,
the single peat brick burning out.
Two nights it roared low and shrieked high; it wasn't
sleep we got, just a burrowing into a dreamcave
that opened out onto this wail,
the clamour that kept finding us.

                                                    My pen froze in my hand, my ink froze
on the page. Salt water in my ball-point pen.
Words, any words. *Eileen Sean and her son Eoine,*
I wrote, *are friends of mine.* I knew this woman,
knew her sisters, even her old
grandmother who had lived just as long as mine, the red
faces, dark eyes and black hair of them all.
*This is craziness,* I wrote. I have fallen into the story
as the boy fell into the water.

## My Great-Grandmother's Hands

Her hands are the blades of two shovels
at the ends of her straight blue sleeves.
The more households she works in,
the larger her hands grow; the more soap and cold water
she plunges her hands into, the redder they get;
the more mahogany knobs she twists her duster around,
the thicker and bluer her veins stand out.
She kneels in church and knots her hands together
like a ship's thick rope tying it to the shore. She longs
to live in a hot country, a country that multiplies
her work with three harvests, a country where
she need never wear gloves, where she can pick
limes and sell them by the dozen in the palm of her hand.
At night she rolls onto her side, slides her cold hands
between her thighs where they will do no harm.

## The Careful Things

Nina, today I ordered a metre
of William Morris fabric, Willow Boughs,
for you – two weeks, it'll take, from England.
We were reverent, the salesclerk and I,
about that old man and his exacting craft
in cotton and wood and paper, but barely
spoke of him or his centenary this year.
The workers' wages, he wrote,
would not allow them to buy the careful things
they made – but Morris would have splurged too.
Pleased with my purchase and wanting
yards and yards of it for my bedroom,
I rode my bike down to College Street

through heavy blotches of rain
in a rainfall too brief to darken the pavement.
A hot wind stirred the sweltering city air,
upward, upward. In the bank with my decisions
I looked out through the glass to see
if the rain still held:
on a courtyard of sorts, the kind you find
on College Street – there, a willow tree shone,
silver leafblades outward,
the green folded inward, away from me.
Fuller and lusher than Morris's, swollen
with heat and withheld rain and fluttering promises.

## Christmas on the Otonabee

Still grey sky, still grey river;
at another year's turning, the snow has failed us
but the scant ice has held fast, at least
from our shoreline to the marsh.

Safe, we think, in the living room,
the Christmas tree blinking behind us
and a cascade of presents unwrapped by dawn,
discarded by nine. All day
the family gathers, mute as planets
in fixed orbits around the TV.
The videos drug us, divert our laughter,
rasping and prolonged, from my niece.
Quiet now, she's learned to keep her thoughts stashed
in a tree trunk by the frozen river.

Mid-afternoon I slip the family knot:
kneeling on the sofa, its weave
the colour and texture of straw, resting my chin
on the sofaback to watch
through the plate glass picture window
two young boys and their big brown dog stroll
– it seems for hours – on the ice.
Walking on the greyness, *walking*
as far as the marsh grasses frozen hard and brown,
walking godlike or buglike
and free of parents.

The daughter in the living room
comes to watch the river beside me,
says she wouldn't trust the ice. Yes,
I nod, still too thin.

# Driving into the Blizzard

**1.**

Early evening on the 115, the long drive home
and the road bares its vertebrae between
the snowdrifts. From the dashboard,
faint pinpricks of green and the clatter
of static between your finger's
*punch* and *punch* at the radio's small face:
blizzard warnings,
but you can't catch the location –
heading here, for us? Flakes
fly up from the road, singly and in pairs.

Your father turns a curve
and a snowblower, big as an iceberg
but loud and sudden, is attacking
the drifts, the car skids, makes a sideways plunge
right for the huge tuba of steel playing
its white noise all across the highway,
spewing sheer white at the windshield.

Afterwards, he can't say which is the worst,
the fear before or during or now;
he tells you his heart is still pounding,
his hands in his old leather gloves
flex and grip the shake out.

Keep him talking into this, out of this,
and soon he is raging against
the highwaymen, that is what he calls them, who
manufactured this unnecessary terror.

**2.**

Robbers on the road
– confront the windshield again
to overpower them: the snowflakes'

relentless blot and bleach in the night

hundreds of blunt chisels
chipping away your memorylode
no choice but to drive into the snowstorm with
the only vehicle you have


3.
Or is this the blur your mother drove her VW beetle into,
into the blankets at the nursing home?
Her twisted brainframe. Aluminum
exonerated, but her memory infects
the whole family. Her soft cheek, her tanned legs.

As your mind stiffens anyway into its age. Arthritic.
Borges, nearing 50, trying to learn Anglo-Saxon,
repeats vocabulary: *used up by years,*
*my memory loses its grip.* The soul's way of telling
him *the universe waits, inexhaustible, inviting.*

Could your memory blizzard into escape, an irresponsible
response to a century's bombings, pamphlets,
its enormous chambers of gas and torture,
and so many armies of young boys, still marching.
The century's quota of cathedral assassinations
filled in the first two decades. Jumbling the precise
sequence, causes, consequences; how many deaths, where, when.
How concealing consoles.
There is no quota.

Or perhaps you have spent too long in the chalkfield
of education, filling in the blanks. Memorize this or mark that.
The poem is writing a multiple choice exam.
Which of the above.

Eduardo Galeano gets on the radio in English, talks about
*recordar*, to remember is to pull through the heart – what
do we have here? cod-jigging through the heart,
a needle and thread
stitching through tough ventricles.
Two weak arms pull on a plummeting chain, a bucket
at the other end, oh, this deep well.
Getting something stuck
in the heart, halfway in, halfway out.

## That night in June at the farmhouse

Sleepless tonight, but the skies have cleared.
Every grassblade beads with twice-fallen
rain: rain now sliding off the willow leaves
onto the rain that fell hard this evening
before I heard of your death. All night
I check on the Big Dipper; hourly it drops
closer to the earth for its scoop of rainwater.
*Can't it stay still?* In the morning
we will leave early, our feet will flatten
trails in the long wet grass to the car.

The
whitewashed
oval
of
a
roadside
grotto

# Event Horizon

*The boundary of the black hole is known as the event horizon ...*
*Events occurring within this horizon cannot be observed ... [and]*
*cannot influence the outside universe.*


A folding yardstick to the stars, a stopwatch
to time the frequency and duration of my visits,
every measure is inadequate to the task
of your care. At task's end is a core burning
itself hollow, an incineration of the two selves,
yours and mine. The physics of the family,
the elderly star reddens and totters on the edge
of the event horizon, generosity implodes within.

It's light-years we've been making this bumpy
bus ride out into the thinning emptiness
of galaxies, the Milky Way is a smear of zinc
skin lotion, pills blot out the stars;
mislaid hearing aids and upper dentures
spin like space junk just
out of reach. This closed and medicated universe, these flying
quad canes, grab bars, aluminum
walkers. Devotion, I believe this is called,
a devotion that unwinds itself through indignities
to death; devotion is the sum of what you wished
for me, its limits and my call.

## Speechless

How to frighten yourself speechless:
hasten to plant the snowpeas
in a morning blur before
a spring trip: open the packet and spill
the seeds: a bounce and clatter
of big beanseeds all over the counter,
the floor: oh, shit: like your words,
in motion, every direction, no control
when you're rushed, not paying attention:
which is nearly all the time: just plant them.

On your return, the squirrels have pulled
every beanseed out of the soil.

Then several mornings later:
something evil, your first
thought: something green and evil
growing out of the kitchen drain's throat:
a slender stalk, five straight inches
up to the light and atop, two wrinkled
leaves unfurling like a tiny
silk bowtie that's been crammed
into a pocket for weeks: forgotten,
insistent: you must remove this:
your own throat tightens: a gentle tug
on the needle-straight stalk: wrong
to keep its pale green here, wrong to pull it out:
fear grows like this, wordless.

## Las Calaveras

*exhibit of Linares family papier-mâché*
*skeletons (calaveras), Fowler Museum,*
U C L A, *Los Angeles, March, 1995*


Today we visited the skeletons, the *calaveras*
in the gallery, papier-mâché families
playing cards, drinking tequila, waiting
for the Day of the Dead to come to life.

We saw how the skeletons had skeletons –
beneath the shiny paint and newspaper: bamboo frames,
the rib and strut and rafter
of the barrel chest, the wasp-waist.
How can we see this art so
clearly, its science and structure,
and yet its life and ours remain mysterious?
Still it works, this helix of molecules
that props our brainwaves up and chains
us into families whether
we know it or not.


Life-size. The art of detail, the bony fingers ringed
and beckoning, the baseball caps and décolletés,
their diamonds and military fatigues.

After an earthquake, the dead can carry the dead
in a stretcher through the rubble, a skeleton can
bleed. They can do everything we can, panic and flirt
and bruise and aim A K 47's.
They are our more vivid sisters, the ones
who were behind us in the family,
our younger brothers, skinny and intrepid, the ones
who want TV's enough to loot them,
our silly cousins and their earnest wives,
rouge on their cheekbones, not their cheeks.

Their foibles only a bit worse
than ours.

Take this ruined quaking city and populate it
with skeletons, have them recover and bury the dead
and play cards after the funeral into the night.
Let them go to the fancy dress ball and afterwards
let them fuck urgently, let them breed
corrupt politicians who will tumble the peso and artists
who will revivify the self-portrait.
Let them create monsters to scare children,
multi-winged iguanas or armadillos whose teeth shine
with green fluorescent paint. Let them go fishing
in polluted rivers and get low-paying jobs
in garment and electronics factories.

They'll come north, wetback
their way to Canada, their papier-mâché
sodden, their bamboo frames arriving on our shores;
with defiant grins, they'll capture
my whole family, throw starched
paper over my mother at her needlepoint,
my father in his wheelchair,
me at my computer, and wrap us all
in the stillness of Pompeii.

# Yellow Parachute

Up there, folded within the cedar chest
on the old stairs' landing, beneath the layers
of fabrics too precious to use – a white silk
monogrammed scarf, the Donegal tweeds and taffeta skirts,
twin christening gowns made out of an old Irish
wedding dress – under all that, lay
the yellow parachute, strings
removed, its flattened wrinkled
texture something we'd never felt before.

The three of us crumpled and smoothed the fabric
– *That's silk*, my mother's reverent nod –
and saw the triple-stitched seams fraying
into petals in the sky. We flung
the parachute open, let it spread
and settle throughout the second floor.
Perfect for two boys to hoist
their younger sister in, to suspend and swing
her in an arc over the stairs below.

Holding my small weight, the yellow silk
was meant to flower with a thud
past the gasping, prolonged, almost-too-late
moment. That moment gaped like the firemen's net while
the women screamed behind and above me,
screamed out of the twelfth, eleventh, tenth
floor windows, and then

me, netted and safe so far below –
deep in the yellow folds, cradled
and slung, I was nothing but a silkworm
learning the lesson of longing,
longing for this game to happen again and again,
wrapping this one instant and carrying it still.

## The High Salt Content of His Tears

The high salt content in my father's
tears, he complains of this, and we check
our smiles. What is the point of gravity here?
Seriously, we ask, your eyes are
stinging? It's the dry hospital air, it's
the sickbed flowers, your tear ducts are failing too,
it's an allergy, you need eyedrops, estrogen,
something. We daub his eyes, we say: Oh well, perhaps;
perhaps in your eighties, your tears
turn oceanic, corrosive.

I lean low over his bed, cup one hand
under his ankle, the other under his knee,
lift and bend his immobilized leg. Press
it in to his chest, right up to the resistance,
lower it. Again, lift up, press to the chest,
lower slowly through the paralysis,
the flaccid muscles shuddering
beneath his skin. Ah, he says,
that's easing the pain in my hip.
Again, ah, so much better now. The ache transfers
to the small of my back, stiffens and holds there.
You're good at this, he says, the pain
has disappeared. No, it hasn't, I tell him, straightening up,
feeling the forbidden knot of refusal tighten.

They're painted blue, these walls, but they only know
how to be green, terrible green from the light
in a bar above his head. The bed is a contraption
for recovery: it whirs and tilts
every kind of discomfort.
Plastic sealers, one-unit doses and servings,
receptacles for used needles, a sign saying
the sharps go in the box
on the wall; no place for the flats,

I tell him. They took it out and threw
it away, he says, but he's talking about his hip
joint. He keeps his eyes closed against the bar
of green light and takes us wandering down
pre-war years, to diagnoses and doctors from fifty years
ago. His eyes fly open when I ask about the day
in his childhood when he scalded himself, a game
he was playing against the old wood stove,
a balancing game he thought he was clever at,
standing on the seat of the pressback rocking chair,
or so I imagine, because he cannot remember
what he was balancing on or testing himself against.
So clever, in perfect control
                                              but just like the rest
of his life, it got faster and more precarious
till suddenly something else was in the balance: a trip
to the children's hospital, bundled into his wagon
and trundled onto the College streetcar.
A scalded leg, the same leg now paralyzed by a stroke,
and a severe nurse who would not whisk the crumbs
out of his bed so that he suffered sleepless all night.
Or perhaps the high salt content of his tears
kept him awake even then and no one to press them away.
The crusty eyes in the morning, the fairy tale
sleep that's lasted a lifetime to wake him
at this moment, another hospital, another injury,
another scalded leg.


2.
At night, someone administers a potion
to me. This is the General, my own anaesthetic,
who has lain atop me all night, smothering my dreams,
shushing my desires, pinching off my fears till
my sleep is a tall straight straw,
bamboo green and leafless, a functional tubing

of rest into my soul. Here,
drink this, says the General, and tips
the draught to my lips, pours it
burning onto my cheeks, ears, neck.
One name, a mother's name, is all that lies
beside me, and there has been a conversation
in the night between a childless woman and
a woman whose children have grown,

                              both longing for
the smoothness of a baby's head here, right
here, and that smell of a sleepy infant
who is about to be laid gently into the crib,
the tentative temporary letting
go that may not work for either of them. The General
is displeased, silences them, awakens me, opens
my eyes to the thin green sting of dawn.

## Old Hall Light

Tonight on my father's street, his front door
stays open all evening, late into the night.
The hall light yellows the linoleum below,
spills onto the porch, down the wheelchair ramp,
aches and glares at us. Here
is a Magritte painting of the rag-edged silence
deep enough to swim into
invented by one lamp on a dark street.

On the sidewalk, my brother and I look back at the house.
Years of filling and emptying,
a tidal flow of toasters and armchairs and uncles,
half-broken or half-mended, depending
on your outlook. I've never noticed
how crooked the hall light hangs. We talk
quietly to our neighbour, *too bad,* we say,
*such a big change,* and *he can't manage anymore.*
We glance back at the hall light;
or ahead, at our own emptying.

## Nine New Undershirts

It was a kind of evasion, the way
I carried that chore past late August,
but his new undershirts for the winter
hardly seemed urgent, the days
still hot and glorious, the nights
not yet ripening to a chill.

Finally, early September,
I bought them, three packages of three
undershirts, low white scoops
at the chest, the armpits, the back,
entirely serviceable, male.
Nine tubes of cotton ribbing, bought
in a hurry, carried around all day,
even left in a washroom for an hour.

As soon as they were laundered and
labelled, he began to die. Two
weeks they sat folded on the windowsill
beside him, and I wondered,
was I bargaining, was I deluded? – *Oh, can't you
just wake up and put one on?*

Now they spill like tissues
out of a bag on my bedroom floor. I pull
them out, wear them one by one, a layer of readiness.

## In Paradisum

When the young man with the odd haircut
stepped to the altar lectern, his tie askew in
a collar that was both gaping and tight,
the organ pipes from the back of the church
rolled forward a deep bass tone
like a wave that crashed
and thinned and finally lapped at his feet.
He closed his eyes and breathed the fading
salt spray up through his brown shoes,
his bony white legs, into his gut and lungs,
right up into his face. In the front row
we took this breath with him; this breath
took less than a second, it was the signal
for the next wave from the organ pipes,
the high reed tone, melodic and sweet,
to make its way to him, for him to open his mouth
and sing *In Paradisum*, the crack of joy
that splits apart the funeral chant, the summons to the angels
to pack this fucking vaulted church and carry
this newly-lightened soul up out of here to heaven.

It was here, at the edge of the ocean,
that I wanted to open everything, open
your coffin and pry open your mouth,
put Charon's coin on your black-bitten
tongue, watch your eyelids flutter and the nodes
of your tongue come alert to the last
taste of the silver I'd rubbed
salty in the palm of my hand.

# Estate

His basement is a soup of rust
and dust and mould; something complex
and burdensome, maybe tears,
has collected in its walls – efflorescence,
the house inspector calls it, normal
moisture, not a concern.

                        Chin-high with decades
of countless hobbies, the debris of production
and avoidance. Aluminum developing pans
heaped with bolts and nails and switches and valves,
porcelain-clad electrical bits, jagged wires
and rubber washers, all baked into an oily stew
too heavy to lift. Spools of soldering wire
whose leaden core I would touch to my tongue
for the quick metallic taste of danger. Unlabelled
jars of seeds, labelled jars of screws and a treasury
of tools: their amber handles, their nicked blades.

Inside the set of tiny green metal drawers
that pull so smoothly on oiled runners,
the cork lining is still scattered with wood shavings
that I pick up, carefully replace. Every bill ever paid
stabbed onto nails on the wall and sixty
electrical cords, each with a plug and one frayed end,
hanging like whips on the back of the door.
Chair-frames, stuffing shredded by mice. Shelves
of hardened preserves. A hundred
bottles of homemade wine, as many old corks saved.
The fire-charred set of cobbler's tools
in a hinged wooden box. Bin after bin
of wood ends and scrap metal, including a pair
of gynaecologist's stirrups. Beneath
it all, lining the baseboard
of two walls are fourteen motors,
their fanblades locked like the antlers

of creatures who'd expired mid-struggle
on this cool, wine-red cement floor.

Here he tunnelled his escapes, carved his returns
to the family. So little he let us hold or name or start;
from each pan, drawer, shelf, I gather one jewel –
drop it into a coffee can
to match the jar of buttons and medals
and buckles and pins
from my mother's estate, upstairs.

# Chac Mool

*Chichén Itzá, Mexico*

We rounded a corner in the ruined city,
found the crumbling statue at our feet;
a boy pointed – *Chac Mool!* in a whisper
both gleeful and urgent: barely submerged
in his gesture and tone, the importance
of horror, how it attracts.

Then my own delight as we sighted another Chac Mool
atop a distant temple pressed against the rainforest,
that recognition: his unsupported recline,
his body in a lying-down S, knees up
and, between his hands, on his slender belly,
the empty dish awaiting the torn-out heart.
A face, as empty as the dish, turned to us,
                asking,
                      What exactly
have you sacrificed your heart for? Whose heart
will you place in my hands, and for
what better good?

I prepare my offerings. First
I hold out my yearnings, bright-red, arterial,
but he is not satisfied, nor does he want
my sins, my sicknesses. When I lean my ear
into his crumbling face, he whispers,
it is your emptiness I want, what is left
behind after the heart is torn away.

                  One after another,
the dark green one, the blue one,
the many black ones, I place in his lap
my father's fourteen motors,
rust-red around their stamped labels.
My hands blacken with the thickness of old oil,

its crust and corrosion, as I haul them
from his basement, two-stroke motors,
the throb and whir silenced, the surround of grief

dense as the rainforest enclosing
the sunbaked square mile of ancient city.

## In the Bottom of the Boat

This morning for the first time
I dreamed you alive again, or barely alive –
there was talk of surgery, I stood at the railing
of your hospital bed; you struggled, gasping
and raging under the toxic fluorescent glare.
First one, then two, your eyes opened
– their blue had deepened –
and you raised your quivering fist at me.
Your arm was too weak, just stirring
out of another stroke, to land a blow. I whispered,
*Why are you angry at me?* In answer
you gathered your lips together
and spit a spray of blackened blood into my face.
I drew back, shamed and aghast among
the hospital staff. Below us, you thrashed
like a huge fish in the bottom of the boat,
hooked on a deathline, something
stronger than me had pulled you in.

The
alphabet
of
what's
given
and
received

# Panorama

*Wilpena Pound, South Australia*

*Click, click, click* all across the horizon,
the landscape artists around me are doing camera tricks.
Cover the entire mountain range with their shutters,
or move in close: all the way up, then
across the reach and spread of a huge gum tree.
Take the photos home, paste them on foamcore,
jigsaw a landscape back into their minds,
onto their gessoed canvases. I cannot
master this freeze, I omit frames and mountains,
make the horizon bump and jitter, my memory
does the same – whole mornings
disappear, names obliterated, the shot
not taken.

# One Corpse

*Wilpena Pound*

Open-mouthed roo at the edge of the trail,
cast aside like an old plush toy
– torn torso, guts bled dry; its tail slit lengthwise,
vertebrae exposed like a musical score.
*You weren't here yesterday,* I think, and hurry past
on the path, cannot bear to look at that open mouth,
the last long breath
drawn past those upper teeth
suddenly, like my father's final sigh.
One corpse among all these insistent anthills,
the dip and swish of the eucalypts' silver leaves.
Above the roo on a big red rock,
a bottle-green lizard
darts one sharp glance over an electric shoulder.

## Fossils, Brachina Gorge

Therese stops the bus, jumps out, *follow me*. Pours water
from her round flannel-striped canteen onto a jut of dull rock.
Spidery red threads appear, smattered veins on an old drunk's nose.
The next grey rock she washes into a smear of marine creatures,
lights them up like a string of Christmas bulbs, red blue yellow green,
hung all along a wire. Scribbles from the sea,
from the bog, from the sand, wedged sideways
and delivered today. The sun disapproves, dries this wild scene
back to the smooth old grey again, stranding us in the gorge
beside a mountain ridge. Covetous, we pick up stones,
spit on them, muttering *five hundred and ninety million years,*
these specks travelling so long, so far without us.

## Stone Sofas

*Brachina Gorge*

Faded pink upholstery, smooth as ironed damask,
a scatter of rocks erupts
in another dry pebbly riverbed, small pools at its edges.
Recline, armchair yourself into these warm pink rocks
— even a rounded cushion, just there, for your aching neck.
Ah, riverbed. Tumult smooths you, those yearly crashing
floods, absent but contained, the evidence
in this living room.

## Cypress Fire

Just before we make the evening fire, a fist-sized knot of wood
falls out of the cypress log. Grey, rock hard,
like a worn old coin with a fading image
pressed into each side: one a singing face,
two wide eyes, a nose, an open mouth,
points of wild hair surround its song. Turn it over
and a lined face with jutting brows, eyes downcast,
a mouth at rest or just about to speak.
Youth on one side; age on the other. Despondency and joy.

In the dark desert chill, the bonfire of non-native wood
is the one red glow for miles; a different tongue
speaking an acrid smoke, its lick and smart
in our eyes, nostrils, throats. A vocabulary
of solemnity or sorrow, like incense.

## After Burn-Out

*Wilpena Pound*

One or two tree-generations ago, in this flat dish of land
rimmed by a thumb-press of mountains, a firestorm
swept up the dry stone river-beds and charred the gum trees
hollow. A massive fallen eucalypt, its white trunk split
away from its base, opens like an eye
I can stand within. How many days of burning
before its trunk and branches hollowed,
crumpled to the red ground? They lie here now, spread
and numerous, like the wrist and bones of a huge hand.

I untie my shoes, take off my socks and step inside the tree,
blackening the soles of my bare feet and my fingertips
against rungs of charcoal, the tree's memory of flame
swirling into its canopy. Walk through this empty black
tunnel to the doorway ahead: into the round leaf-strewn room
where the roots held firm in the firestorm and, knuckled
into the dry riverbank, speaking thirst, replenishment,
sprouted four green stalks.

## Sand Dunes

Fine sand pours like floodwater into my boots
as we climb the huge red sandbanks. At the top, I ask
the few straggles, the long-stemmed plants,
yellow flowers and silver-blue leaves, *Crotoleria
eramea*, what are your many names? Above us,
the sky is a solid grey felt mat, so close we could
hook it with our fingertips, pull it down
over us. But turbulence churns in two far corners of the sky —
storms are approaching from both directions.
I sit and watch the wind erase our footprints,
ripples forming around them in the dunes.

## Desert Rainfall

Tent pegs bent, pounded crooked into this hard-pan
desert floor. A cloudscrim's
pulled between us and the stars
— if it rains, we break
camp in the night. Warned
and waiting, I lie sleepless
in my blue tent, an eyelid
squeezed tight against the sky.

As slow as a pulse
the rain begins. How can it fall
this slowly, this singly,
never quickening? And no one moving
in the other tents. This is like waiting for a death,
a birth. At some agreed-upon degree of dawn,
we all emerge head-first, squinting
from each tightly-zippered slit.
The sandy clay ground is barely wet,
but in minutes our footprints are picked up
and walking away with us.

## The road closes and opens

Off in the low western sky, one oval cloud
like the eye of God follows us along
this road which is sealed and unsealed in patches and streaks;
hitting the red is going internal, entering
the continent's throat and guts.
After two days and three nights
of slow spare rain that thins to a hanging grey,
the red dust road
swells to clay, thickens our bus tires
for a rear-wheel slide on a chewed-up track
– but then the eye shuts and vanishes
in a wash of blue, and the bare road opens, drying
in the steady new glare of the sun.

## Corrugated Iron

I learn about it from the paintings.
I don't notice it in the cities, towns, the outback
till I see it in Drysdale's landscapes. Then
everywhere. Curls of wavy iron
littering the scrub, the outback:
like metallic tree-bark
peeled from roofs and fences and modest middle-class homes, lifted
and ripped and corner-dented by the wind. Abandonment
and solidity, the fragility of human plans. I search out
tin-roofed sheds, perfect sheltering rain-drums, each drop
amplified. I open my camera lens wider
for the grey-blue metal, lift the horizon
up high, enlarge the red foreground to take it in.

# Junk Jewellery

*Gammon Ranges, Mutawintji beyond us*

Search for bottles in the old inverted cubes
carved into the earth, cellars fallen in. Find heel cleats,
perfect letter D's. Horseshoes, square-head nails still attached.
Flowered china shards, the whole porcelain rim
of an old bedpan. C and D and O, the alphabet of settlement
printed onto the landscape and abandoned. Fragments.
Re-arrange far-flung sardine cans, keys
still attached, in a perfect straight line on the desert floor.
Stow the prizes in the bus:
one dark green bottle, whole but warped, caved in
– melted in a fire;
a tiny corked medicine bottle, faint blue, salt-stained;
a dented kerosene can, its matte-rust
roughened into the desert's gritty red.
In the sun, brown bottles soon turn
a mottled purple – not as old as they look,
not special. But their sheen. I pick up
a thick pale green circle, sharp chipped edges
just beginning to smooth: the bottle's base, a medallion.
Close my fingers around it, press it into my palm.
Jewellery of the household. The desert's
huge fist holds it all, crumbles it
back into rust, into silica, into sand.

## Broken Glass

Fourteen days of gazing into the long red horizon
and each day at this particular late slant of the sun
the glitter of broken glass burns our eyes.
All this shatter across the continent, I collect it like shells, the sharp
chips, the smooth discs, washed like driftwood by the desert sand;
the purple, the brown, the green and the soft iridescent blue.
Nothing to do out here, says a traveller,
but take your gun and shoot your beer bottles into smithereens;

when I tell him how, each night, the glass on the cracked red ground
scorches into my dreams, he kisses me suddenly, deeply –
a kind of blessing, an award for the last thing I see before falling asleep.

## Target Practice

Today the wind sings over the outback,
slides up an eerie empty scale; wavers at the top, a wail
covering the scrubby landscape like a fragrance.
Its song drops a pitch, tears down the road from the abandoned hotel,
and in the distance, lifts,
lassoes a knot around the brick tower
at the boarded-up gold mine, its extinguished hopes.
The moan widens again, pours over the high slag heap
and off into the horizon. Then returns in slivers, shrill and sustained,
an unceasing cry.

Hours of this, and we walk far up the sandy road, find the roadsign's
aluminum post speckled with bullet-holes.
The wind blows across the pole's hundred
torn lipholes: a metal reed, its many keys of desolation.
We stopper the holes with our fingers,
we play the wind, its thin wounded chest, target practice.

The
first
three
times
were
scorching

# Horoscope

*A shy acquaintance finally warms up to you. All your fears*
*are unfounded. Money troubles ease up. Prepare for a trip.*


O my sister & brother Aquarians, one-twelfth
of this city population,
we can abandon fear, give up
therapy, thereby smoothing the cash flow –
now we can call Aer Lingus & Cathay Pacific.
Our worries are pyramids crumbling from within;
the breath of admiring tourists has unstuck
their hieroglyphs. History & curses are harmless,
I hum a new tune in my kitchen, chopping the okra. The water
in my pot finally warms up to me, I add the cornmeal
& parmesan, stir for half an hour: all on its way to polenta,
to share with a shy acquaintance.

## Upside-Down Cake

My upside-down cake tilts
like a dreidel on its point.
'Must be home-made,' say the friends,
the well-wishers. 'They don't let
cakes like that out of the bakery.'

Ah, but they get out on their own.
They lean in a certain direction, towards
the oven door, towards the birthday,
the candle heat. Lopsided with wishes
they make their escapes.

Imperfect birthday cake, perfect
formation of something about
to spin. About to say something
centrifugal, something planetary.
Perhaps what it wants to say will be
eclipsed, torn away. Bitten into.
Something secret will happen
in the half-dark, and when we are allowed
to look again, not a new
star, not a new piece of metallic
space junk but something flashing
from what was about to be spoken
and what finally was spoken
behind the moon's back.

This is how tremendous changes
can take place, the tilt and twirl:
irons in the fire, separations and tsunamis,
flashfloods and geological
cracks in the plates as they stand crowded, lined up
at the back of the china cabinet.
In there with the bone, oh god, bone china cups.

# Clang

Quick, throw on your coat and run outside because all the bells are
ringing – this is war's end, happy marriages for all and a plentiful harvest
fused into sound – ; ringing as if the despot had been dethroned, the lost
recipes for kindness found, earthquakes and calamities dispelled
from the land. All of them, all at once, seem to peal from everywhere! Run

to the bellcot, never mind the hard westward slants of grey rain – lift your
    face
up into the chimes glancing off every aspen leaf, fencepost and vole. Watch
    the bells tilt
and scatter buckets of O's in every direction, they are birds' mouths, opening,
    filling,
opening again. If you want to ring like a bell, you must ring from your core
to your fingertips, scalp, your hardened soles: wholehearted – it's dangerous
to rattle just the clapper from within, you will crack like early ice on a lake,
a huge piece missing thereafter like the five-ton Russian bell.

Stay for the fade, the one long note again, again, again – its ache and
residue; joy is still in our repertoire, and we,
perversely, wish it gone.

## This, then, is the snow-filled track

This, then, is the snow-filled track
I have trudged to your cabin door,
the awkward bliss of these long strides
into the one set of footsteps ahead of me.
And then your greeting, grim and distracted.
Another misjudged visit. Tramp back, obliterate
my own careful footsteps, smash them into a path.
So that was hope back there, that
indiscernible flurry in my heart.
Pine needles loosen their grip, clumps of snow
slip off the boughs. To the north of us,
ice cracks across a glacial lake:
the drowned city stirs once, sleeps on.

## Cold Feet Hotel

Early morning under the long icicles,
skidoos are scattered in pairs like the slippers
of giant winter gods around the lakeside hotel.
Sheathed in leather or nylon
for the night, single headlights
hooded: each skidoo rests its eye, its fierce
winter heart. The lightest snow
falls, barely a dozen flakes a minute

into the cedars, into the late sunrise
spilling pinks across the blue snow.
The lake is large and not yet frozen;
desire's still asleep in the bush,
her eyes lidded with a thick snowcrust.
Year's end approaches, daylight dwindles,
and I await the snowgods' roaring
and stamping, screeching us all awake.

# Lip-Synching, Two Performances

*You're innocent when you dream.*
*– Tom Waits*

1.
We hear his tenor voice before
we catch sight of him. *Glory*
*to the land,* his song scratch-needles
through the winter air. Packed
snow on the boardwalk, our muffled
footsteps, the inattentive
mountains all around us.

Our boots tramp closer: three men,
one miming song for another who
videotapes him; the third one, shivering,
holds the CD player.
Top volume now,
we have misheard *Glory to the lamb.*

Behind us all, the smooth face of the hotel
rises like a dream from the frozen lake,
a face resting on its pillow.

2.
In her dream, she is singing
the words to the song I wrote in my dream.
Its lyrics were the thick carpet in the hallway, your
shoulder leaning against the doorframe,
your arm held out, your lips suggesting
a kiss that would pull anyone to the floor.
The two planes of the kiss and no goodbye.
It was summer, you were dressed entirely in
magician's silk. Our bodies' certainty, taking
those high notes and staying there just
inside reckless.

She sings the same long touch
in the ramshackle dream
hotel, its burgundy
carpet and yellowing lampshades. Unhesitating,
no rehearsal, just the kiss and its applause.

3.
We mishear the song yet
take it for our own, as she took
that kiss and replayed it with her mouth:
borrowing this force, this utility. How
song, not sex, digs deep into the lungs,
soft tissue, cells; hides
in the cortex, survives stroke and aphasia
and dementia. *Daisy, Daisy, give me your answer, do,*
those nursing home songs are the only things
that stir them to smile, not
food, not touch, not family.

Isn't this what a song is for, the singing
again and again? The body learns it
by giving it away over and over, each time
pitching it at perfection.

# First Symptoms

## 1. consultation (interior)

In the disorder of my thoughts a lowgrade
fever of conversation with you spikes, an underlay
of throbbing: this, now out
in paperback; this, an escarole soup
recipe to give you; this piece of gossip
about an acquaintance. Silence is not
the problem. That old, old poem
about a cloud
passing over the face of the mountain.


## 2. consultation (exterior)

But measure in tiny tastes your name taking shape
on my lips. In the darkness, my head on my pillow, I count –
your name wanted out
how many times in today's conversations? Silence
is the problem. That old, old poem.


## 3. charting

How it works, this sudden interest
in calendars. Vigils, marches
lectures and movies: events to share.


## 4. fanning

Smiling, I suddenly hug
my colleague who spoke up in her meeting.
Impetuous warmth. Certainty flickers, glows.

## 5. precautions

Careful but frequent phone use: match but
don't exceed your calls. Permissible questions,
impermissible suggestions. Rules dense
as a thicket; scrambling, I gash
my arms and legs. Thorns and thistles,
they grow up from where? But must be obeyed.
A tablet of commandments that only I know.
Or that everyone but me knows.
Slit the wall of brush that as quickly
grows up behind me. I have rested
in this small clearing before, long ago. And here,
brookside, where I washed the dried blood
from gashed ankles and pressed at wounds to feel
for infection. Legs bound up again for the plunging.


## 6. gauze

How easy this is, spiderwebbing: spinning
these conversations with you. These skeins
and filaments, almost strong
enough to skip across now.


## 7. treatment

As with all the other illnesses,
attention and courage, several doses daily,
given and taken orally. Pick up the phone's blue
receiver.

## 8. Do not smile

Sakanoe writes, Do not smile to yourself
like a green mountain
with a cloud drifting across it.
People will know.

## When the face of the former beloved

When the face of the former beloved
visits you in a dream just before dawn,
her shoulder leaning into the doorframe
a shrug hardened against the oak,
when you look so close into her face
greeting her and wondering if she's been sent
unwillingly into the dream,
this is a day troubled at the edges.

When her face – unsmiling, her dark eyes,
her pink lipstick – hovers all day like a mirror
in front of the desk at your ill-fitting job,
just an eyelash above all the phone calls and memos,
and still she's giving you nothing but her beauty,
a wistful fog settles all through your report.

And if, in your dream, you have chatted dangerously
to her about pre-nuptial ceremonies
in the Asian sub-continent, dream-facts
you have concocted about a mother splashing
water on her daughter's naked thighs
before inscribing her palms with henna patterns,
if you have twisted those rituals into a coil
of desire that tell her *Prepare me again*,
then you need a graceful
exit from the dream, not your own lame laughter.

When you feel the face of the former beloved
like a scarf drawn across your eyelids just before waking,
there's an odd peacefulness, a tranquil
recognition of what she's still able to say
even across the distance of the years
and the several lakes between you.

When you awaken like that, you pull
the night fragments winding-sheet tight

as if they were warmth,
you let your thoughts bleed underground again,
seeping under the working day, faxes
and meetings and return-that-call.

There's an odd rightness to it all:
what you've been waiting for,
her clothes scattered on your hotel bed
just there, behind you, just like before.
It's you that's gone visiting,
stopping again for a night and a day
like personal leave for an out-of-town funeral
and returning to work, distracted, wrung out, full.

## Six Tulips

Six tulips, seven kisses; nine days
they've lasted. A yellow flame at the core
of each red star brightened in my living room
as the first days collected; the petals
softened wider, lacking an embrace
to hold them still, fix
them into this room. The air
has bruised the petals a slow purple
at their edges. This affliction called time,
I complain to them.
                        Nine days' absence
and I am searching for the messages
written with this reaching
and shrivelling: all these curled petals,
deeply red, scattered around the glass of water,
and six green stalks, ready as pencils
to mark this paper
with their crow-black pollen.

## What Dreams Assume

When she was trying to convince me
to part with a small shred of my self, a tooth or
a bone in my toe, the dream assumed my integrity
and my body's wholeness. But laid bare
the incompleteness of my resolve.

Dreams assume you are multilingual,
that you can understand the body's conversations
with botany and architecture and food;
that you are familiar with fancy dress balls,
comfortable in yellow chiffon. The dialects of colour.
You visit country after country,
but most are called the Netherlands.
Dreams have a way with names.

The two keys, wish and fear, do not always fit
precisely into crusted old keyholes, but dreams know
who jammed the lock with a needle.
All your life you are collecting keys, looping them
on an old chain clipped to your belt.

Dreams do not value originality, especially in forms of danger:
they expect you not to laugh
at being a maiden tied to a railway track
rescued by a married man at work
who knows electricity as well as he loves you.

They assume you want to see the recently dead
smell their body scents, hear the precise timbres
of their voices, but they will withhold those pleasures until
you have stopped longing for them – then
send you a suitcase with your friend's
brown leather jacket, the label slit away from the satin lining.

They have an understanding about vases on a high shelf,
how they can change into extinct Chinese animals

with slow blinking eyes. They expect you not to hesitate
at the swimming pool's sting when its water
is replaced with soy sauce, deep,
saltier than any ocean.

Dreams tally your expectations and failings,
assume you will encounter your fears
with equanimity, but will generously make you
as small as a turtle whose mother was a butterfly.
They assume some insects have parents of different species,
that flowers are occasionally mechanical, hiding tiny mirrors
that require adjustment, repair. Or that birds
need exercise and will devise watery contraptions
for providing it.

They reckon you have no legal training –
without charges or counsel, they send you to trial,
imprison you, sentence you to death. Escaping,
you race breathless towards awakening, daylight's reprieve.

Dreams do not suppose that you live in this century, or this body.
They do not care about your precise age,
what gender you have been reared into,
and when you are in danger, they assume your attention
is elsewhere. They suspect you need to consider
your part in your father's death. They have their own anatomy
of the foreign and the familiar.

Like poetry, dreams know more than you,
the entire field, figure, ground and foreground
and your solitariness therein.
Dreams believe there is a remedy,
they always know where to begin,
with the enlargement of the catastrophe all the way to Hiroshima.

Dreams themselves are fond of sleeping,
unaffected by your petitioning and your patience:
this casts doubt on your sincerity.
They dislike being aroused, stalked or
captured in a net upon waking – this is why
they are sometimes sullen and punishing,
make you cry out or gasp in terror,
or why they rebel, sitting for months by a deep volcanic lake.

## Two Weak Arms

Two weak arms: how to be useful still,
now that I can no longer row a boat
any distance at all, carry a child
upstairs at bedtime, or even tap lightly
at the keys for very many hours.

In this weakness Rapunzel's story revisits me,
its earlier version: how later tellings
suppressed her twin sons
who fled the tower with her
into the desert, awaiting their blinded
father's return. Am I being asked now
to survive as the tale has,
simplified,
the two voices muted,
and carrying less love, less truth?

Here in this boat where I pause, mid-lake with you,
caught in the lake's green net with its mirroring rim
I pull up the heavy oars, my back
to my destination: my destination is a tiny
reflection in your eyes. Straining
to what point on its shore, this
is our discussion, while the waterbugs
stitch quick weightless arcs on the surface.

Moving will help, but so will staying still.
Listen, hold the two boys in your arms
as I begin the story again.

## Lunar Eclipse

Tonight the earth like
a faithless lover wins back
the moon with the extravagance
of a last-minute gift: throws
her a pair of black silk stockings.
This pleases her, she smiles
a one-sided smile at
the expensive ink pooling
at her feet. She swirls
a toe in the sheer
fabric, stirs and un-
stirs it into loops on the sky's
floor. Considering. Then slowly,
utterly slowly, she takes an hour
to slip into them.
Her gift is the donning of the gift.

We have stayed up
for this, not expecting
reconciliation. I am phoning
friends all over the city,
putting aside grudges, making
amends, saying,
*Stand in your window to receive this.*

# Notes on the poems

The epigraph is from the title poem in Marianne Moore's *What are Years?* (1941) in *The Complete Poems of Marianne Moore*, New York: MacMillan Company / The Viking Press, 1967.

page 19, 'Waterman's Fountain Pen'. Some of the imaginings about this soldier's life are taken from details about Amadeo Modigliani's Paris days noted in the Montreal Art Gallery's Modigliani exhibit in 1997.

page 24, 'Irish Literature Exam'. The story referred to here is a re-working of one told in *Peig: The Autobiography of Peig Sayers of the Great Blasket Island,* trans. Bryan MacMahon. Dublin: the Talbot Press, 1973.

page 29, 'Driving into the Blizzard'. The poem by Jorge Luis Borges is 'Poem Written in a Copy of Beowulf,' translated by Alastair Reid from *The Self and Other* in *Selected Poems 1923-1967,* ed. Norman Thomas Di Giovanni, Delta, 1968. The quote by Eduardo Galeano is from an interview with Eleanor Wachtel on *Writers and Company,* C B C, 1995.

page 35, 'Event Horizon'. The definition of this imaginary sphere surrounding a black hole is from *The Oxford Concise Science Dictionary*, Oxford University Press, 1991. Boyce Renberger, in *How the World Works* (New York: Quill, William Morrow, 1986), defines it similarly: 'Within the sphere, or event horizon, matter continues to shrink, but we can never detect what is happening because the event horizon marks the boundary within which gravity is strong enough to keep in all light and radio waves.'

page 37, '*Las Calaveras*'. The Linares family of Mexico City has, for several generations, created papier-mâché skeletons on a sculptural scale. The exhibit of their work at the Fowler Museum (the University of California at Los Angeles) in March, 1995 documented an extraordinary social history as well as exquisite craftsmanship.

page 48, 'Chac Mool'. I have used here a commonly-held (though disputed) interpretation of the Chac Mool statues at Tulum and

Chichén Itzá in the Yucatan Peninsula of Mexico. Some writers
maintain that in Mayan ceremonies, 'elderly men called *chacs* cut out
victims' hearts with an obsidian blade,' anointed statues with the
blood, and flung the corpse down the temple steps; the victim was
flayed by the priest and the remains eaten by the spectators, except for
the hands and feet, which were reserved for the priests (Mark J.
Dworkin, *Mayas, Aztecs and Incas: Mysteries of Ancient Civilizations of
Central and South America,* Toronto: McClelland and Stewart, 1990).
Others maintain that this interpretation is 'scandalously false' and that
'the statue represents a priest or deity lying down on its back with bent
knees. It holds a four-rattle square with a solar disc in the centre. It
expresses the idea of heaven with one rattlesnake in each corner'
(Adrian Gilbert and Maurice Cotterell, *The Mayan Prophecies:
Unlocking the Secrets of a Lost Civilization,* Shaftesbury, Dorset:
Element, 1995).

page 76, 'First Symptoms'. Poem by Lady Omuchi of Sakanoue, in *The
Penguin Book of Japanese Verse,* trans. Geoffrey Bownas and Anthony
Thwaite, Harmondsworth, 1964.

page 82, 'What Dreams Assume'. This poem was inspired by these lines
in Louise Gluck's poem, 'condo': 'I hate when your own dreams / treat
you as stupid' in *Vita Nova,* Hopewell, N.J.: Ecco Press, 1999.

# Acknowledgements

My thanks to the editors of the following journals and anthologies for accepting earlier versions of these poems for publication:

*Arc*: 'Harm's Way'
*Canadian Woman Studies*: 'Irish Literature Exam'
*Contemporary Verse 2*: 'Precaution'
*Descant*: 'Lie perfectly still. Turn on the light'; *'Las Calaveras'*
*Dig.desire*: 'Lip-Synching', 'Two Performances'
*Fiddlehead*: 'Upside-Down Cake'
*Garm Lu*: 'Irish Literature Exam'
*Grain*: 'Clang'
*Literary Review of Canada*: 'The molecular level of kindness'; 'Yellow Parachute'
*Our Times*: 'The High Salt Content of His Tears'
*People's Political Poem Winter Contest, 1999, finalist*: 'Storks of Kampala'
*Pottersfield Portfolio*: 'In Paradisum'
*Prism international*: 'Speechless'
*Southerly (Australia)*: 'Junk Jewellery'; 'Fossils, Brachina Gorge'


*Riprap: Fiction and Poetry from the Banff Centre for the Arts,* ed. Edna Alford, Don McKay and Rhea Tregebov, Banff Centre Press, 1999: 'Harm's Way'; 'Precaution'

*The Edges of Time,* ed. Maureen Whyte, Seraphim Editions, 1999: 'Dance Pavilion'; 'That night in June at the farmhouse'; 'Christmas on the Otonabee'

*Vintage 99*, League of Canadian Poets Anthology, 1999: 'Two Weak Arms'; 'Chac Mool'; 'What Dreams Assume'

*Vintage 97/98*, League of Canadian Poets Anthology, Quarry Press, 1998: 'When the face of the former beloved'


My deepest thanks to Miss Vickie's Writing Mistresses (Linda Briskin, Jennifer Rudder, Liz Ukrainetz, Barbara Young), Joanne Page,

Kathryn Payne, Sheila Stewart, and Jane Springer who commented on this manuscript; special thanks for help with the cover art to Jennifer Rudder. I am grateful to Diane Mah, who invited me on a camping trip for landscape artists to the Australian outback, and to the wonderful artists who inspired me with their laughter and their art.

Thanks also for the careful editing and encouragement from faculty at the Banff Centre for the Arts during the early stages of this manuscript: Don McKay, Jan Zwicky, Erin Mouré, Rhea Tregebov. Thanks to Tim Lilburn, Sharon Thesen and Paul Wilson at the Sage Hill Writing Experience. More thanks still to Roo Borson, especially for the help with the Australian poems, to Elisabeth Harvor and to Betsy Warland. And thanks to Sandy Thorburn for help with musical terminology and concepts. I thank all of these readers for helping to shape individual poems or the overall concept of the book. And finally, my warmest thanks to Barry Dempster for his supportive editing and unfailing good cheer.

Some of these poems are for friends: 'Upside-Down Cake' is for Liz Ukrainetz; 'Irish Literature Exam' is for M.H.; 'What Dreams Assume' and 'Two Weak Arms' are for Ann Bjorseth; 'The Careful Things' is for Nina Spada; and 'That night in June at the farmhouse' is in memory of Margot McGrath-Harding.

Maureen Hynes is a Toronto poet whose book, *Rough Skin*, received the League of Canadian Poets' Gerald Lampert Award for best first collection of poetry in 1995. With Ingrid MacDonald, she co-edited *we make the air: the poetry of Lina Chartrand* in 1999. Her poetry has appeared in journals across Canada and Australia, as well as in many anthologies. She has also written *Letters from China* (Women's Press, 1981). She is poetry editor for Our Times magazine and a community college faculty member.